METALLIC &LUSTRES

By Hugh Giese

SECOND PRINTING

Published By:
©1993 SCOTT PUBLICATIONS
30595 EIGHT MILE
LIVONIA, MI 48152-1798
ISBN# 0-916809-69-2

No. 3507-11-93   PRINTED IN U.S.A.

INTRODUCTION

Lustres and Metallics are probably the oldest form of overglaze decorating, having begun somewhere around the 9th Century AD in Persia. Some of the most beautiful plates and tiles which are preserved in our museums are wonderful examples of this type of decoration.

There are other families of overglazes such as china paints but they do not resemble each other and have different properties and applications. Most overglaze families can be used on the same piece but do require separate firings between applications. Fired china paints can be covered with lustres but they do have a frosted finish when fired.

Lustre decoration is also one of the most frustrating and at times, aggravating of all ceramic techniques. Variation in application or in the firing process can make all the difference between a beautiful work of art and something that at times is ready for the trash can. One consolation, however, is that in many instances, the piece can be salvaged by either burning the material off at a high temperature or covering it up with a darker colored lustre.

TYPES OF PRODUCTS

We usually separate products into metallics and lustres for convenience sake. The metallics are Liquid Bright Gold, Liquid Bright Palladium, Liquid Bright Platinum, Red Copper, Gold Bronze, Chinese Bronze and Gun Metal. These products are made from various metals and are held in suspension by different oils. They are very volatile substances before firing and therefore subject to evaporation unless kept in a tightly closed container. They all have the same dark brown appearance before firing, so it is necessary to make sure that your bottles and lids are labeled correctly.

These metallics, when fired, are basically opaque as compared to the colored lustres which are either transparent or semi-transparent after firing. Metallics also become part of the fired, glazed, surface when fired to maturity whereas lustres remain on the surface and will wear off after constant use. It is suggested that lustres be used strictly on decorative rather than utilitarian pieces.

For instance, tannic acid from tea will sometimes turn the inside of a lustred cup to a brownish color. Acetic acid (vinegar) will sometimes eat off the lustred surface of a plate, or knife and fork marks will scratch the surface. Lustres are also not recommended on ashtrays because the heat of a cigarette will sometimes mar the surface.

Most lustres are lead safe when used over a lead safe dinnerware approved glaze so there is no fear of contamination when used on certain types of china or ceramic pieces. With overglazes as well as other types of materials, however, it is always best to check labels.

Mother-of-Pearl is the most well-known lustre and gives a very delicate rainbow effect. Many ceramists think only of Mother-of-Pearl when thinking of lustres but there are many others. Blue Pearl gives a light blue irredescence while Green Pearl is similar with a delicate light green appearance and is often used on Christmas trees. Amber Pearl fires to a light amber that can be deepened with multiple applications and firings. Rainbow Opal is another favorite of ceramists and is similar to Mother-of-Pearl only more vivid in color.

Wild Dove is a gray-brown lustre and can vary in coloration depending on application. If a very thin coat is applied, it will result in a light tonality and the heavier it is applied, the darker it will become. Wild Dove is excellent when used over an underglaze that appears unevenly applied. It has a tendency to minimize the uneven underglaze application.

Blue Storm is a dark blue lustre and is very effective in itself or applied over fired Liquid Bright Gold or Liquid Bright Palladium, which gives a carnival glass finish.

Avocado Lustre is the gray-green of avocados. It is a neutral color that can be used on leaves and is especially effective over crackletone glaze. Black Coral has a very lustrous sheen and has the color and high gloss of the Black coral in the Hawaiian Islands. If applied too thin, it will have a brownish cast but can be given another application to deepen the color.

Golden Sky when fired is the color of the sky on a sunny day.

Sea Green is a dark grey-green with a suggestion of blue as an undertone. When used over fired gold, the result is a green-gold tonality.

Blue Lagoon is a beautiful blue-green lustre, the color of the deep pools in south sea island lagoons.

Purple Clouds when applied with regular, even brush strokes, results in a shiny deep purple. If applied with a circular stroke an uneven cloud-like effect can be achieved.

Fabrique is a clear Belleek lustre that gives opalency without color as found in the beautiful Beeleek china of Ireland.

Northern Lights has a blending of lavender, pink and soft gold. It resembles the flashing aurora borealis of the far North.

Golden Earth fires to a light brown lustre similar to Wild Dove. It too changes when applied heavier or with several applications with firings in between.

Burnt Orange fires to a deep, rich orange color and is marvelous on pumpkins.

Because one lustre un-fired, can contaminate another, it is imperative that you mark not only the vials but the caps as well so there can be no mistake in re-capping. Lustres should be recapped after pouring an amount that you plan to use into a small container. This method lessens the danger of contamination of the whole vial. This procedure will also delay congealing of lustres.

THINNER

Thinners are used for diluting any of the materials in case of thickening in the bottle and also for air-brushing techniques. Products from the manufacturer are normally at the proper consistency but they do have a shelf life and if left until they thicken, problems may develop.

Lustres and metallics are not suspended in water. They do have a suspension agent that is subject to evaporation. Thinners are made for just this purpose and only a drop or two is needed to bring them back to the proper viscosity. If they pull too much however, they will flow away from your brush which can spread them to cover a larger surface.

To help avoid evaporation we suggest placing a small square piece of plastic wrap material over the opening of the bottle before placing the cover back on. Make sure that the caps are also tight to prevent this evaporation.

When thinning products do not do it in the container (vial). Take a small amount from your vial with the tip of a palette knife cleaned in denatured alcohol and place it on a glazed tile or saucer that has also been cleaned. You may then use your thinner a drop at a time to achieve the proper consistency. The reason we suggest this method is to help eliminate contamination. If you have to discard a bit of color on a tile it will not be so bad but if the whole bottle must be thrown away it can really be expensive.

APPLICATION

If you know you are going to apply metallics or lustres on a piece you should apply one more coat of glaze to the piece than normal. Then fire the glazed piece as close to cone 04 as possible. This will aid in firing out imperfections that might hurt the overglaze finish later. You should note that lustres and metallics do take on the surface texture of the glaze over which they are applied. Matte or satin glazes give a dull finish while gloss glazes will produce the traditional high gloss finish.

First and foremost, when using metallics and lustres you MUST work in a DUST AND DRAFT FREE area. Dust and moisture are the two most detrimental elements in working with metallics and lustres.

Assuming that a better than average application of glaze has been fired to maturity, the first step is to clean the surface of the glaze with a cleaner to remove any dust, finger-paints, or grease-like coatings sometimes found on the ware after glaze firing. Any of these things can cause metallics and lustres to pull away, or separate, resulting in bare spots or white areas on a finished piece.

DO NOT work in a room where there is cooking or boiling liquid. Even smoking in a room will leave little bits of moisture in the air. Coughing and sneezing is also not recommended while working, so if you feel the urge, get up and away from your work area. Air conditioning may also cause moisture to be in the air. Hot, humid days can also affect the materials.

Thin, even applications of lustres and metallics are a must. If a deeper color is desired, then re-apply the material being used and refire. Never pat a spot, but go over the entire area and refire.

The piece to be decorated with lustres should be at room temperature, not hot out of the kiln. If they are not allowed to cool off the decorating job will be extremely difficult. The oils would evaporate so fast that the lustre would become too sticky to be handled.

When doing a large all-over surface with metallics or lustres, start in one spot and then work a little bit to the left and a little bit to the right, so that when you finish on the far side of the piece you will meet "wet" with "wet". Otherwise you will get an overlapping and too heavy an application in this area and the result will be a burn off or dull effect.

Begin with a brush full of lustre (see thinning) and remove the heavy drop from the tip of the brush on the side of your palette or color container before applying to your piece. Metallics should be applied in a smooth, even stroke and working quickly so that overlapping does not occur.

Lustres are usually applied in a small, swirling or what I call a "C" stroke. When replenishing your brush, do not start again directly on top of where you left off. Leave a small space in between and then work the material **back** to the line of demarcation. Continue around the piece until you meet on the far side.

Speed is very important to lustre painting. Lustres dry very fast and if too much time is spent in the decorating operation, heavy rings could form and this would be very unattractive. Slight unevenness will always develop in application but you should not try to get it out as it will even out when drying. Do not put the piece in a warm place too soon or the oils in the lustre may evaporate before any unevenness has a chance to disappear.

When working on a heavily detailed piece make sure that the lustre does not pool in the deeper crevices. Always brush out the excess material in the recessed areas before it dries and continue working.

Lustres do not mix or blend therefore you are restricted in some of your work in attempting to create naturalistic work. Lustres can be applied over one another as long as you fire in between. You can create some beautiful effects by doing so. You can apply more than one color to a piece per firing but the colors cannot touch.

To obtain deeper and richer tones you should ap-ply two coats of a lustre with a firing in between. You are better with two firings since too heavy an application of a lustre will cause it to chalk or powder off.

Metallics, such as gold, copper, platinum, etc. will sometimes show cracks if applied too heavily or fired too hot. Metallics should be of a rich, deep carmel or straw color when applied. If they are underfired, the results will not be the pro-per color, often appearing dark, rather than bright, clear metal. As a test, rub the fired metallic with your finger to see if any of the color comes off. If it does, refire to the proper cone and often the problem will be corrected. (Please see section on firing.)

When you have com-pleted application of any metallic or lustre you should store the piece in a dust free area or in a con-tainer that will not allow dust to penetrate.

BRUSHES

Square camel hair or sable brushes are recom-mended for applying metallics or lustres. They should not be any larger than 3/8" but this size would depend on the size of the piece you are doing. Soft brushes are best for the smooth, even coverage necessary in overglaze decoration. In order to keep your brushes in a clean usuable condition we recommend that you adhere to the following pro-cedure in cleaning your brushes.

First take a small amount of brush cleaner or one of the thinners in a small glass jar and swish the brush around to remove most of the material from the brush bristles. Then wash gently in soap and water. Next take some **clean** brush cleaner and follow the same routing. Do this three times: cleaner, soap and water; cleaner, soap and water and finally, cleaner, soap and water. Place the brushes in a dust free container so that they are clean the next time you want to use them.

It would be ideal to have a separate brush for each of your lustres and your metallics but this is not always possible. If you have a limited supply of brushes make sure that the brushes are clean and thoroughly dry before using them again. Remember, moisture is very bad for lustres and metallics.

Sometimes after firing one of the lustres a small bluish area will develop on a finished piece. This is due to a dirty brush so make sure that you clean your brushes before you put them to bed for the night.

If this situation does oc-cur, you can fire the lustre off by firing the piece to the maturing temperature of the glaze. Many times metallics will not fire off completely but the lustre can be redone and refired.

If your brush sheds a bris-tle or two in the application process and it lodges on the piece, be sure to remove it before firing. If left, a blemish will be created on the finished piece.

SPECIAL EFFECTS

Weeping Gold and Weeping Platinum are special effect metallics that produce a fine web pattern when applied properly. Use as large a brush as possible (according to the size of the piece) and place a brush full at the top and brush in a vertical, or in an up and down stroke. Then continue in this same manner until the entire piece is covered. Used over a clear or white glaze there will be drops and feathery runs of gold over a lavender pink background.

Remember! When gold is not applied heavy enough or you smudge the metallic in application, a pink-purple stain will appear after firing. This stain can be removed however, by using a commercial product known as "Gold-Off" or with a Gold Eraser. Many times when using Weeping Gold, you may want to remove the pinkish cast and just leave the fine webbing of gold.

Some of the dark colored lustres are also effective on certain pieces which have been dispersed with Weeping Gold or Platinum. Both of these products are applied in the same way. Use as large a brush as possible and use an up and down stroke.

There is another product called Fantasy that produces special effects but is applied in a slightly different way. After wiping down the piece with glaze cleaner allow the piece to dry for about 15 to 20 minutes. Brush on a very thin coat of either Gold, Blue or Silver Fantasy and allow to dry for a few minutes. Then with a small round brush, touch a small amount of the Fantasy product to the surface and you will see little ringlets separating the material. Depending on the size of the brush, large or small circles can be achieved. An overlapping effect is desired in this technique rather than a polka dot effect. If you desire colored Fantasies, apply any of the colored lustres in the regular way and then place the dots or circles on the wet lustre using one of the Fantasy products.

Other special effect products include marbleizer, Metallic Flo-Base and Antique Etch.

Marbleizer is usually used in conjunction with metallics. To use this apply Liquid Bright Gold or Palladium or Platinum on a colored gloss glaze and allow it to get tacky dry, usually about 20 to 30 minutes. Then with a large, clean brush flow on a good coat of marbleizer. Do not press down too heavily with the brush. This media produces a film that dries and as it does dry, cracks and forms a fine webbing of metallic over the colored gloss glaze. Allow to dry. Firing will produce cracks allowing the background color to show through. You may wash the brush used for marbleizer with soap and water.

Metallic Flo-Base can be applied in a heavy coat to a cleaned glaze surface and while the material is still wet, place small drops of Liquid Bright Gold, or any other metallic and the Flo-Base will cause it to run into interesting patterns. Some of the dark colored lustres can also be added for additional interest. Just remember to apply the metallics or lustres to the surface while the Flow-Base is still wet. It can be used on vertical, concave, or convex surfaces which permit better flowing. Spinning the metallics or lustres on with a banding wheel on top of the wet Flo-Base can also produce interesting results.

Antique Etch is used on a low fire greenware surface to create craters either with an eye dropper or fairly large, round watercolor type brush. You can continue to reapply the etch material to give additional depth of the erosion or control it in certain designs. It is excellent for the old, dug up look of buried artifacts. When firing this material do not place it next to a piece in the kiln that has glaze on it. The fumes from the etch will affect the glazed ware.

Lustre Resist is manufactured by some companies as well and is used for blocking out areas that you do not want lustred. All areas, except the part to be lustred must be completely covered. The lustre is then added. The resist will fire away.

AIRBRUSHING

Most lustres are of the proper consistency for airbrushing without thinning. You may want to add a drop or two of the proper thinner when working with metallics however. This gives you a better flow of the products through the airbrush. I also recommend using the fine tip assembly on the airbrush when working with these materials.

Use thinner for cleaning the controls before drying them thoroughly. In this manner, your airbrush equipment will stay in tip top condition. Do not use these controls for anything but metallics and lustres the same as you would not use your regular brushes for any other materials.

ONE WORD OF CAUTION: When airbrushing metallics and lustres work in a **well ventilated area** or with a spray booth set-up. Also do not have any sparks from motors, the heat of a kiln, no cigarette smoking or pilot lights in the area because materials when airbrushed are combustible.

You do want your piece slightly warm for this application as you want the color to dry as soon as possible. Stencils are commonly used with an airbrush to create designs using lustres and metallics however, many simply use the airbrush for all over, shaded coverage.

OTHER APPLICATORS

Although brushes are the most commonly used means of applying lustres and metallics there are others. You may use a sponge, pen, stamp, roller or other tools as long as they are cleaned properly to prevent contamination.

Stamping is usually accomplished with a rubber stamp design. Gold is spread on a tile with a palette knife, allowed to thicken slightly and then used like ink to decorate.

Sponging uses the same thickened material and is simply dabbed on the ware. Special effects along borders or patterns can be created using this dabbing motion. For different patterns use this same motion and lamb's wool, silk or even steel wool as an applicator.

FIRING OVERGLAZES

You can take all the precautions in application and have clean tools to work with, but unless your piece is fired properly your results will be unsuccessful. The proper temperature for the type piece and media, plus ventilation, are the most important factors in firing.

The standard firing temperature for lustres and metallics is a cone 019-018. When given a two cone temperature number such as this it means for you to use the higher cone temperature in your kiln if you have an automatic shut-off. In this instance 018 is the higher temperature indicated. When using lustres or metallics on glass use cone 022 or 021.

The idea in firing is to attain a high enough temperature to obtain proper adherence of the lustre or metallic to the ware. If underfired your decoration will wipe off, if over fired it will sink into the glaze and lose its brilliancy or burn off all together.

As mentioned, ventilation is imperative to firing. Normal kiln operation when firing lustres or metallics is to turn the kiln to low for an hour with the peepholes and lid propped open. This is followed with another hour of the kiln turned to medium and the lid open two inches throughout the entire firing process. The kiln is turned to high about an hour later but the lid is still propped open and the peephole plugs remain open. The kiln will turn off quickly as the low cone temperature will be reached rapidly. Allow to cool at least as long as it took to fire.

These times may vary depending on your kiln, the power input you have and how fully loaded your kiln is. The important thing to remember is to leave the lid open long enough so all smoke and gases have escaped. If in doubt, leave the kiln on lower settings longer. If you have created a masterpiece be sure to test fire before attempting the primary job.

It is recommended as well that you do not fire anything from another overglaze family such as china paints with overglaze colors. They may require the same cone but one could contaminate the other. Do not place pieces too close together to allow for the required ventilation and distribution of heat. If you load your kiln with more than one layer of pieces do not shut off the ventilation for the bottom pieces. Do not load pieces too close to the side walls or elements either.

If you don't already know it, you will soon learn that strong fumes are generated during the firing process which is the evaporation of oils within the metallics and lustres. The smell annoys some people so you will need to ventilate the room and may have to fire when the room is empty or on a weekend.

You may note during firing that the pieces turn black. This is normal and will disappear at the proper time, allowing the proper color of the finished ware to come through.

Firing is an extremely important part in using lustres and metallics but it is not difficult if you follow the precautions outlined. Many times the overglaze is faulted when the glaze used softens more than required and causes crazing or other defects.

It is suggested that you make test firings anytime you are using a new product. This will not only insure your success but it will also help you determine the characteristics of the products and equipment you are using.

OVERGLAZE FAULTS

Let's discuss some of the pitfalls and problems that you may experience when working with metallics and lustres.

Lustre chalks off during firing:

This is caused by applying the lustre too heavy, especially in the crevices of highly detailed pieces. Be sure to allow the lustre to dry before firing.

Dull gold:

When working with metallics do not go back over the unfired areas thinking that you did not apply it heavy enough or see a thin spot. If you notice brown areas on your pieces instead of the rich carmel or the straw color, this is because you went back over it, and when fired, this area became dull in appearance. It can also be caused by poor ventilation that allows fumes to settle on piece.

Metallic rubs off after firing:

This is due to not firing it high enough and/or poor ventilation.

Small white spots after firing:

This is caused by moisture which has attacked your piece.

Black specks in lustres:

Caused by dust or contamination on the piece.

A large black spot appears on the piece after firing and will not fire away.

This is called a "hardspot" in the piece and is usually caused when pouring the slip into the mold or from excessive cleaning in one area. When coating the piece with glaze it will be very thin where the hardspot is. When you apply a lustre it turns black on this thinly glazed area. To help eliminate this you can use a small amount of vinegar in your water when cleaning greenware as well as apply a heavier coat of glaze to pieces.

Crazing:

If the bisque was fired too soft to begin with it will cause a glaze defect. If it is the glaze lustres will crack in long lines. If the cracks are sharp lines, in a spiderweb fashion, the fault is in the lustre which is caused by too heavy an application.

Purple or blue spots:

In gold it can be caused by too thin an application. In Mother-of-Pearl, it is probably contamination. You can correct by applying more gold and refiring but you have to fire off the lustre and start again.

Circles in overglaze:

This fault looks like a circle along the underlying glaze to show through and is caused by dust or line on the wet surface of the piece. Can be caused by grease, oil or moisture.

Tiny bubbles or pin spots in the ware:

A blemish of this type will be overly accentuated, especially when metallics are used. However, this is a fault in the glaze, not the overglaze. Could even be a fault in the original greenware.

Mother-of-Pearl appears to be dull:

This can be caused by too hot a firing (or too long a firing cycle) or if the lustre is applied too heavy, but not heavy enough to chalk off. Poor ventilation can contribute to this also.

Crystals appear in lustres:

Usually indicates too much heat, however, if the lustre is too old the same condition may also appear, but it is rare, however.

SPECIAL TECHNIQUES

Metallics and Lustres by:
Med-Mar Metals

Goose Ring

MATERIALS NEEDED:
Suitable greenware
Underglazes:
   Light Green
   Mustard Gold
   Black
Light Grey One-Stroke
Transparent Matt Glaze
Wild Dove Lustre

Brush three coats of the Light Green underglaze to all of the grassy areas of the ring. Mustard Gold underglaze is then brushed on in a three coat coverage to all of the beaks and feet of the geese. Bisque fire to Cone 06-05.

Thin down some of the Grey One-stroke slightly with water and brush one coat over the entire piece. Wipe down the Grey coloring with a slightly dampened sponge leaving the color in the deeper crevices. Allow to dry thoroughly and then brush on two coats of Transparent Matte Glaze. Fire again to Cone 06-05.

A very light coat of Wild Dove Lustre was then applied over the entire piece, or if you want a more even coverage, airbrush or spray the lustre on the piece. Fire to Cone 019-018.

(Note: When airbrushing or spraying lustres or metallics, do not have any cigarettes burning, no kiln firing or any pilot lights going in the spraying area. The materials are combustible when sprayed, so be cautious in this respect.
NOTE: Mold by Holland Mold Company.

Stations of the Cross Pitcher (See Cover)

MATERIALS NEEDED:
Suitable greenware
Black One-stroke
Clear Gloss Glaze
Liquid Bright Palladium
Mother of Pearl Lustre

After cleaning the greenware, bisque fire the piece to Cone 06-05.

To the bisque, brush one coat of the Black one-stroke, thinned slightly with water over the entire outside surface. With a damp sponge, remove some of the color from the highlight areas. To avoid smudging of the color, keep turning the sponge to a clean section and keep rinsing the sponge.

Pour glaze inside of the pitcher with Clear Gloss glaze that has been slightly diluted with water. Allow to dry thoroughly and then brush two coats of undiluted Clear Gloss to the outside surfaces. Fire to Cone 06-05.

Wipe the piece down thoroughly with a Glaze Cleaner or Acetone. Do not use rubbing alcohol. Allow the piece to dry about 15-20 minutes and then apply Liquid Bright Palladium to all of the heavy arches of the design, the rim of the lip, the base and the handle. Fire to Cone 019-018. (Note: When applying metallics or lustres, start in a small area and work a little bit to the left and a little bit to the right, so that when you reach the far side of the piece, you are meeting wet with wet.)

Wipe the piece down once again with Glaze Cleaner and then apply Mother-of-Pearl Lustre over the entire outside surface, including the fired Palladium areas. Re-fire to Cone 019-018.
NOTE: Mold by Kentucky Mold Company.

Elephant Box

MATERIALS NEEDED:
Suitable greenware
Clear Gloss Glaze
Silica Sand
Liquid Bright Palladium

This technique can be adapted to many different greenware shapes, but I thought it especially nice on this unusual elephant box. I have also done nativity sets in this technique as well as several oriental items.

After cleaning the greenware, bisque fire to cone 06-05. Pour glaze inside of the lid and the box with Clear Gloss Glaze that has been thinned slightly with water. Allow to dry thoroughly.

Add a small amount of silica sand into some Clear Gloss Glaze which will give it some texture. Make sure that it is still a brushing consistency. Brush on three coats of the textured glaze and then re-fire to Cone 06-05.

Apply Liquid Bright Palladium over all outside surfaces, working a little to the right and a little to the left until the entire surface is covered. Fire again to cone 019-018.

NOTE: Mold by Grem Mold Co.

Blue and Gold

MATERIALS LIST
Suitable greenware
Underglaze:
  Medium Blue
  Dark Blue
Lustre Resist
Liquid Bright Gold
Banding Wheel
#4 Bristle Fan Brush
#4 White Bristle Square Brush
Airbrush or spray equipment

Thin down the Medium Blue underglaze by taking a full jar of color (2 oz.) and a half jar of water. Shake thoroughly to mix properly. Spray this color in an even coverage all over the entire outside surface of the piece. Just go over the areas about twice. Keep back away from the piece about 8 to 10 inches so that you do not develop a build-up of color in any one area.

Trace the pattern to the greenware by using Graphite or Mylar paper and make sure that your underglaze color has dried thoroughly before doing so. The pattern can be traced vertically such as you see pictured, or horizontally on a different shaped piece.

With the #4 White Bristle Square Brush, wipe out some of the color in the blossoms and add a little white highlight in the leaves as well. Outline the entire pattern with the Dark Blue underglaze and then bisque fire the piece to cone 06-05.

Pour glaze inside of the vase with diluted Clear Gloss Glaze and then spray Transparent Matt Glaze to the outside surface. Thin down the glaze in a 2/3 Glaze to 1/3 water proportion. Be sure to wear a mask over your nose and mouth when spraying glazes because they are a toxic material which should not be inhaled.

Keep back about 8 to 10 inches from the piece and go over the surfaces at least five or six times to insure adequate coverage of the glaze. The true test when spraying transparent glazes over an underglaze color is to let the piece dry thoroughly and when you can just barely see color coming through, then you have sufficient coverage. Fire again to cone 06-05.

Apply Lustre Resist inside the blossom and leaf designs and allow to dry thoroughly. Don't get too much of the material on so that it develops drips or runs on the piece. Allow to dry thoroughly.

Place the piece on a banding wheel, making sure it is centered on the wheel. Put a small amount of Liquid Bright Gold on a clean tile and with your #4 Fan Brush, spin on some of the Gold Metallic all over the outside surface of the piece. Using the Fan-type brush you want the spun effect, so do not fill in the metallic in a solid coverage.

Peel off the Resist, or allow it to fire off. Fire again to cone 019-018.

NOTE: Mold by Fres-O-Lone Mold Co.

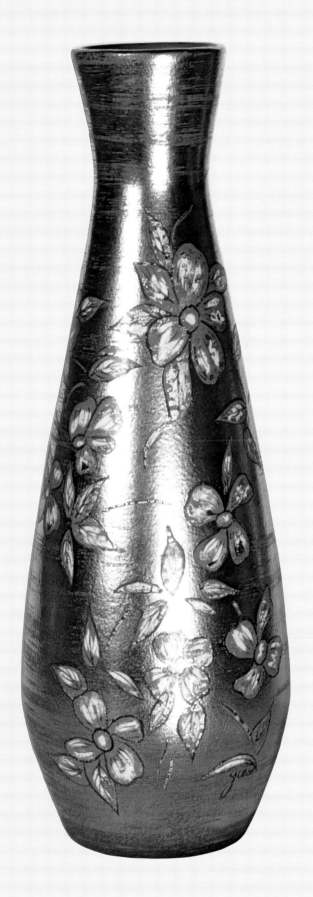

SIDE 1   SIDE 2

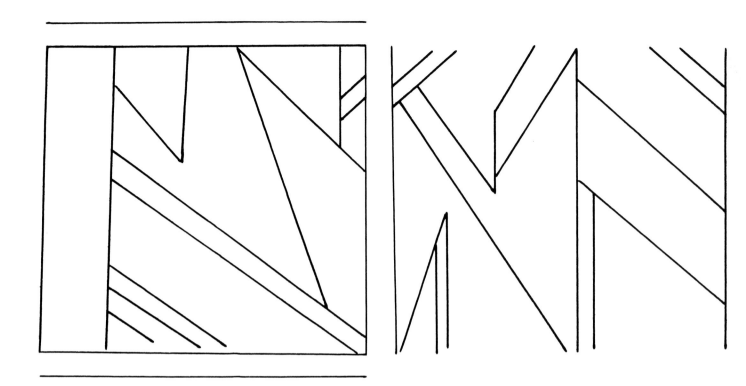

SIDE 3   SIDE 4

Contrast in Textures

MATERIALS NEEDED:
Suitable Greenware
Dark Brown Texture Glaze
  (one with silica sand)
Yellow Satin Matte Glaze
Dark Brown Gloss Glaze
Liquid Bright Gold
Golden Earth Lustre
Avocado Green Lustre
Burnt Orange Lustre
Antique Etch
Sgraffito or Loop tool

This is a very versatile mold because it can be used as a planter, or if you cut out the top area as indicated in the mold, it can be used as a tissue box cover. The geometric design is traced to the four sides of the piece starting with the #1 section and continuing around the piece. Make sure that your connecting lines of the design join each other as you go around the corners.

Incise the lines of the design in the greenware by using a blunt sgraffito or loop tool. Do not make these lines too fine, make them bold. Then apply an Antique Etching material to certain smaller portions of the design as indicated on the pattern. This will crater the surface of the greenware in these areas. Bisque fire to cone 06-05.

To the top and bottom bands, apply three coats of a Dark Brown Texture glaze. On the center design area, including the Antique Etched surfaces, brush three coats of a Light Yellow Satin Matte Glaze. Three coats of the Dark Brown Gloss Glaze is brushed inside of the planter and then glaze fired to cone 06-05.

Apply Liquid Bright Gold to the Yellow Satin Matte areas working left and right after you have wiped this area down with Glaze Cleaner. Fire again to cone 019-018.

To the areas which you created with the Antique Etch, apply Golden Earth Lustre on top of the fired Gold in a thin coat coverage. Allow this to dry thoroughly before using Avocado Green and Burnt Orange Lustres over the other fired Gold areas. Alternate these two lustres as you work around the design area. In other words, all of the fired Gold should be covered with another color of lustre. Re-fire to cone 019-018.

NOTE: Mold by Holland Mold Co.

Basket and Candlesticks

MATERIALS NEEDED:
Suitable Greenware
Clear Gloss Glaze
Northern Lights Lustre

After carefully cleaning the greenware, then bisque fire all pieces to cone 06-05. Apply two generous coats of a Clear Gloss Glaze to all pieces and fire again to cone 06-05.

Wipe the pieces down thoroughly with Glaze Cleaner or Acetone and allow to dry at least 15-20 minutes before applying the lustre.

Northern Lights Lustre is then applied in a very thin coat application. Start in one section of the basket and work the lustre a little bit to the left and then a little bit to the right in a small swirling or "C" stroke. In this way, by the time you come around to the far side of the pieces, you will meet "wet" with "wet" and eliminate an overlap of the lustre.

Do the same with the candlesticks and then fire the pieces to cone 019-018.

NOTE: Molds by Holland Mold Company.

compote

outside of
the piece, including the red
berries. Fire to cone 06-05.

Wipe the pieces down with
Glaze Cleaner and after allowing it to air dry about 15
minutes, apply the Liquid
Bright Palladium to all of the
leaves and the heavy border
design area on the lid and side
of the jar. Low fire the
Palladium to a Cone 022 and
then scrub off the border
areas only by using a cleanser
such as Ajax or Comet. Wash
the piece off thoroughly so as
to remove any of the crumbs
from the cleaner and when
dry, apply Wild Dove Lustre
over the entire outside surfaces. Wild Dove is a Lustre
that has a tendency to get
darker when applied heavily,
so make sure that you have a
thin, even coverage of the
Lustre. Fire again to cone
019-018.

*NOTE: Mold by Indiana
Mold Co.*

Small Llamas and Tiki

MATERIALS NEEDED:
Suitable greenware
Clear Gloss Glaze
Transparent Matte Glaze
Sea Wool Sponge
Black Coral Lustre
Liquid Bright Gold
Relief Mask or Wax Resist

This is another project in contrast of textures. . .using a Gloss Glaze together with a Matte Glaze. Where the Metallic or Lustre goes over the Gloss area it will be bright and shiny. When it is over a Matte Glaze, the overglaze will be dull. Depending on the shape of the piece, this technique can also be done with other Metallics such as Red Copper, Chinese Bronze, Gold Bronze, or Palladium.

With a dampened sea wool sponge, print the Relief Mask or Wax Resist on the green-ware. Make sure that you do not squeeze the sponge to close up the large holes and do not hit at the piece. Simply veil the masking material all over the outside surfaces of the piece. Allow to dry thoroughly. Then, brush on two coats of Clear Gloss Glaze. Naturally the glaze will absorb into the open areas of the greenware and will not take where you have applied the mask. Fire to cone 06-05.

Brush two coats of Transparent Matte Glaze over the entire outside surfaces. Here again, the Matt glaze will absorb into bisque, but not on top of the Gloss glaze areas. Re-fire to cone 06-05.

On the Llamas, I applied Black Coral Lustre for the contrast of dull and shiny and Liquid Bright Gold to the Tiki. Fire these to cone 019-108.

NOTE: LLama molds by Tesoro Molds and Tiki mold by Crest Molds.

Woman of Beauty

MATERIALS NEEDED:
Suitable greenware
  poured in Stoneware
Clear Gloss Glaze
Liquid Bright Gold
Airbrush equipment

Metallics and Lustres can create some unusual effects when applied over stoneware or porcelain, so I thought it only fitting to include one project done with this high fire material.

Cast the greenware using stoneware slip which is fired to cone 4, to cone 6. This happened to be a light beige tonality, but any color will suffice.

Bisque fire the pieces to cone 6.

Apply two coats of Clear Gloss Glaze to the flesh area only on the head. The design is also done with Clear Gloss Glaze and a small detail brush. Fire the pieces again to cone 6.

Thin down a small amount of the Liquid Bright Gold with a few drops of Gold Thinner and then airbrush the metallic over the entire surfaces of the pieces. By spraying the color on, you achieve a smoother application of the overglazes. A word of caution when airbrushing with Metallics and Lustres...do not have anyone smoking a cigarette, no kiln firing and no pilot light from heaters on because the materials are combustible when sprayed. Fire the pieces to cone 019-018.

You notice that where the gold is applied directly to the stoneware bisque it is a very dull color and of course over the Gloss Glaze areas it is bright and shiny.

NOTE: Woman mold by McNees Mold; Platter mold by Schmid Mold.

Foo Dogs and Jug Vase

MATERIALS NEEDED:

Suitable greenware   Clear Gloss Glaze
Ice Blue Gloss Glaze   Liquid Bright Gold
Christmas Red Glaze   Marbleizer

Both of the techniques pictured here are done the same way. The only difference is that the color of glaze is different.

To the bisque Foo Dogs, brush on three coats of the Ice Blue Turquoise Glaze and fire again to cone 06-05. The vase is done with three good coats of Christmas Red Glaze fired in a well-ventilated kiln. By a well-ventilated kiln, I mean that you leave the lid of the kiln propped open at least two hours after you turn the switches up to High and it reaches a white-hot heat inside. Also, do not place the peephole plugs in on a Red firing. Fire the Red glazed piece to cone 07-06. . .in other words, a little bit lower temperature.

Wipe the pieces down thoroughly with Glaze Cleaner and allow to dry before applying Liquid Bright Gold all over the outside surfaces. Allow the Gold to get "tacky". . .which takes anywhere from 30 minutes to 45 minutes. Then with a large Mop-type brush, apply the Marbleizer over the entire piece. As this dries, it will begin to crackle the Gold. Allow to dry thoroughly before firing to cone 019-018.

Pumpkins

MATERIALS NEEDED:
Suitable greenware
Green Hi-Tone (undercolor)
Clear Gloss Glaze
Avocado Green Lustre
Burnt Orange Lustre

Pumpkins are traditionally done in either an Orange Glaze or an Orange Opaque Stain. Why not try something different for a change and do them in Lustres?

After bisque firing the pieces to cone 06-05, brush one coat of the Green undercolor which has been slightly diluted with water to the outside surfaces of the pumpkins... including the stems. With a damp sponge remove some of the color by streaking the pieces in a vertical stroke. I usually apply my color in the same direction that I am going to wash off the highlights. Keep turning the sponge to a clean section and rinse the sponge often. Allow to dry before pour glazing the inside with Clear Gloss Glaze that has been slightly diluted and then brushing on two coats of undiluted Clear Glaze to the outside surfaces. Fire to cone 06-05.

Wipe the pieces down with Glaze Cleaner and be sure not to fingerprint the pieces once you have them wiped down. Apply a thin coat of Avocado Green Lustre to the stem and when thoroughly dry, apply the Burnt Orange Lustre in an up and down stroke to the remainder of the piece. The Burnt Orange Lustre has a tendency to become darker with a heavier application... not too heavy though so that the Lustre will flake off after firing. Start in one section and work a little bit to the left and a little bit to the right so that when you come around the far side of the piece, you are meeting "wet" with "wet". Allow to dry and then fire the pieces again to cone 019-018.

NOTE: Mold by Ox Mold Co.

Unusual Effects

MATERIALS NEEDED:
Suitable greenware
Clear Gloss Glaze
Blue Satin Matte Glaze
Burnt Orange Lustre
Blue Storm Lustre
Metallic Flo-Base
Liquid Bright Palladium
Banding Wheel

The vase pictured is a one-of-a-kind project. You can duplicate the coloration but you'll never get two exactly the same. After the bisque firing, pour glaze the inside with a slightly thinned down Clear Glaze. Roll it around the inside quickly and out. Remove any drip marks from the outside with a damp sponge. Allow it to dry thoroughly and then brush on two coats of undiluted Clear Glaze and fire again to cone 06-05.

Place the vase on a banding wheel and make sure it is completely centered. Prepare all of the materials needed because this is a very fast technique. You will need in addition to the Burnt Orange Lustre, Blue Storm Lustre, Metallic Flo-Base, two fairly

Continued on page 27

large round watercolor brushes and a large mop-type brush. Pour a small amount of the Lustres on separate glazed tiles along with the brushes. Brush on a heavy coat of the Metallic Flo Base on the outside of the vase. Then, **while the material is still wet,** get the wheel moving and band on the Burnt Orange Lustre, skipping about 1½" to 2" between bands. Drop that brush and pick up the other one and place bands of Blue Storm Lustre in between the others.

Keep your wheel spinning all the time until you have all the bands on the piece and then stop the wheel. The Flo-base will pull your colors downward into an unusual pattern. Allow to dry thoroughly before firing to cone 019-018.

The round planter below is another method of getting unusual effects. After glaze firing the piece with three coats of a Blue Satin Matte Glaze, get yourself a large bucket...large enough so that the piece will go down inside it. Fill the bucket about

three quarters full of lukewarm water. Flow some of the Blue Storm Lustre on the top of the water and then some of the Palladium. Muddle them with your spatula but not so much that the overglazes will sink to the bottom. Keep them floating on top of the water as you swirl the planter down through the lustres. Remove from the bucket and allow to dry thoroughly before firing to cone 019-018.

NOTE: Vase mold by Boyer Mold Co. Planter mold by B & C Mold Co.

Modern Decanter

MATERIALS NEEDED:
Suitable greenware
Clear Gloss Glaze
Suitable decal
Golden Sky Lustre
Golden Earth Lustre
Airbrush equipment

After firing the piece to the bisque, pour glaze the inside with diluted Clear Gloss Glaze and then when dry, brush on two good coats of undiluted Clear Gloss Glaze to outside surface. Fire to cone 06-05.

Select a suitable decal and place it in a tray of tepid water. As soon as the decal begins to curl up in the water, remove it and place it on a glazed tile. DO NOT LEAVE the decal in the water because there is a sizing on the paper backing of decals which is necessary to adhere it to the glazed surface. Once the decal begins to open up again, it is ready to slide off onto your ware. Place a few drops of water on the piece where you are going to place the decal, so that it will be easier to position it before it sticks to the piece. Squeegee the excess water from the decal by starting in the center and working to the outer edges. Don't press too hard or you may tear the thin back paper of the decal. Make sure there are no wrinkles underneath the

design area and allow to dry thoroughly before firing to cone 019-018.

Wipe the piece down with Glaze Cleaner and then you are ready to apply the Golden Sky Lustre. Once again start in one spot and work a little to the left and a little bit to the right in short, small "C" strokes. The "C" strokes are important in bringing out the color in your lustres. Allow the piece to dry and then airbrush the Golden Earth Lustre to create a frame around the piece and enhancing the colors in the decal. Fire again to cone 019-018.

NOTE: Many people ask me if they can apply the Lustre on top of the decal before firing. This is not possible because there is a paper backing on all decals which must burn off first. Decals are by Ceramics Unlimited. Mold by Wilson Mold Co.

Candle Holder

MATERIALS NEEDED:
Suitable greenware
Matte Crackle Glaze
Turquoise Translucent Stain (oil base)
Wild Dove Lustre
Liquid Bright Palladium

To the bisque piece, brush two coats of Clear Gloss Glaze on the inside of the candy box and lid and to the outside, brush three coats of a Clear Matte Crackle Glaze. Fire the pieces to cone 06-05. Wipe the pieces down with Glaze Cleaner.

Brush the Wild Dove Lustre to the outside surfaces of the pieces with a short "C" stroke in a thin, even coverage. Allow to dry thoroughly.

Then, take a small piece (3" x 3") of heavy gauge plastic, crinkle it up to create some sharp edges and then paint Liquid Bright Palladium in an all-over coverage. Just lightly touch the piece rather than hitting at it. Fire the piece to cone 019-018.

Brush on one coat of the Turquoise Translucent Stain all over the outside surfaces and remove this with a piece of t-shirt material. Wipe until dry. This will bring out the cracks in the Crackle Glaze. Dress up the candleholder with a matching candle.

NOTE: Candleholder mold by Stangren Mold Co. Candy Box mold by Fres-O-Lone Mold Co.

Dragon Planter

MATERIALS NEEDED:
Suitable greenware
Clear Gloss Glaze
Sea Green Lustre
Burnt Orange Lustre
#4 Fan Brush

This is a fairly simple technique and can be used on many different shapes and forms that are heavily detailed.

To the bisque, brush two coats of Clear Gloss Glaze to the outside surface after pour glazing inside. Fire to cone 06-05

Wipe the piece down with Glaze Cleaner making sure you get down into the detail grooves of the design.

With a fan brush, drybrush the Sea Green Lustre from back to front in a horizontal stroke. Allow to dry thoroughly and then do the same with Burnt Orange Lustre from front to back. Just lightly touch the piece with the bristles of the brush for the best effect. Allow to dry and then fire to cone 019-018.

NOTE: The dragon planter mold is by Fantasy Mold.

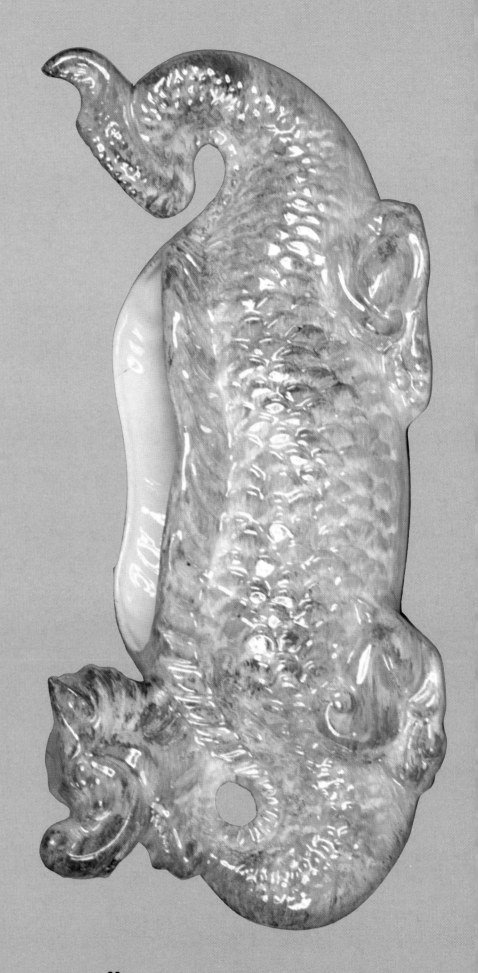

Flower Plaque in Metallics

MATERIALS NEEDED:
Suitable greenware
Onyx Black Satin Matte Glaze
Liquid Bright Palladium
Red Copper
Gold Bronze
Gold Thinner
Airbrush equipment

After cleaning the greenware, bisque fire the plaque to cone 06-05. Brush on three coats of the Onyx Black Satin Matte Glaze to the front and back of the piece. Make sure the Glaze does not build up in the deep crevices of the design. Fire to cone 06-05.

With the #5 tip assembly in your airbrush, apply the Liquid Bright Palladium to all of the leaves of the design. You might have to add a few drops of Gold Thinner to the Metallics to avoid spattering of your color. Clean out the control of your airbrush by flushing it with Gold Thinner, soap and water, three times around, the same way you would clean out your regular brushes.

Once you have cleaned the control, just run air through it for about a minute to help dry up any moisture. The large blossoms are then done with the Red Copper and the smaller ones with Gold Bronze. Make sure you clean out your control each time before going on to the next Metallic. Once more a word of caution when airbrushing with these materials, they are combustible when sprayed, so no cigarette smoking, no kiln firing and no pilot lights in the room. Airbrush a small amount of the Red Copper and Gold Bronze around the outer edge of the plaque also to help frame it. Fire the piece to cone 019-018.

NOTE: Mold by White Horse Mold Co.

Unicorn Box

MATERIALS NEEDED:
Suitable greenware
Birch Gray Satin Matte Glaze
Clear Gloss Glaze
Liquid Bright Gold
Weeping Gold
Gold-off

Glaze the bisque pieces by brushing on two coats of Clear Gloss inside the box and the lid and three coats of Birch Gray Satin Matte Glaze to all outside surfaces. Fire to cone 06-05.

Apply Liquid Bright Gold (or Palladium) to the Unicorn and the small grassy area on the lid of the box. Low fire the piece to cone 022. Make a paste of a kitchen cleanser and remove some of the fired Gold from the highlight areas of the Unicorn. Make sure to wash the piece down to remove any crumbs left from the cleanser.

Apply Weeping Gold (or Weeping Palladium) to the plain surface of the lid and the bottom section of the box. This is applied in an up and down stroke with a fairly large brush. Fire the pieces again to cone 019-018.

Take a small amunt of Gold-off on a paper towel and remove the pinkish stain that develops from under Fired Gold. The separation into an interesting web pattern occurs as the piece is drying before the firing.

NOTE: Unicorn box mold by Atlantic Mold. Co.